HEARD IN ART

Ekphrastic poems broaden and deepen our understanding of their subjects; only the best ones, however, match their visual eloquence. In Hoyt Rogers's marvelous new volume, *Heard in Art*, time and again, whether addressing works from Titian or Vermeer, Tintoretto, Caravaggio, or Claesz, sublimely, with wild erudition, they do.

—Daniel Lawless, author of *I Tell You This Now*

After all is said and done, whatever it is we leave behind of ourselves can sometimes be deemed an extraordinary treasure. This exquisite collection of ekphrastic poems—*Heard in Art* by Hoyt Rogers—based on a favored grouping of paintings by the artists Titian, Tintoretto, Caravaggio, Claesz, and Vermeer, is just that. With great imaginative zeal, Rogers reveals those particulars within each work that might easily go unnoticed but which are fundamentally critical to the balance of each painting. His poems accompany each depicted object and each character by way of an eloquent association of its details with his own hopes, dreams, loves, and regrets. By doing so, the artist and the poet have traded places. The painting has become the poem, the poem has become the painting, and with deepest thanks to Hoyt Rogers for his keen ear, both are the gift we're given to hear.

—Paul B. Roth, author of *Before the Aftermath*

Hoyt Rogers has bravely chosen famous paintings, supreme masterpieces, to explore in his sequence of poems. Bravely but also wisely, because readers fortunate enough to discover the book will bring their own love and knowledge of the pictures to these encounters. The highest praise I can give is my certainty that our mutual mentor, Yves Bonnefoy, would have loved this magnificent volume—not only the poems, but the generous notes as well.

—Anthony Rudolf, author of *Silent Conversations* and *European Hours*

Paintings do not speak. They show. Such is the paradox announced right from the title of Hoyt Rogers's captivating *Heard in Art*. The poet has carried off the tour de force of listening to painting, that "silent poetry" (as Simonides of Ceos put it). Through his precise, vivid, indeed sensual poetic language, the very settings and scenery, the objects and finery, the models and their truths or fictions, appear themselves to be asserting their presence. And Titian, Tintoretto, Caravaggio, Claesz, and Vermeer can somehow be heard passing over in their minds how each detail must lead to another and form a visionary whole. Yes, the spectator—the poet, but also the reader—is "a seer" who has learned to listen to "the seen." This is Baroque illusionary art at its subtlest and often at its most verbally lavish: these ekphrastic poems are miraculously expressive.

—John Taylor, author of *What Comes from the Night*

HEARD IN ART

Ekphrastic Poems

on Titian, Tintoretto, Caravaggio, Claesz, and Vermeer

Hoyt Rogers

SPUYTEN DUYVIL

New York City

© 2025 Hoyt Rogers

ISBN 978-1-963908-81-7

Book design by T Thilleman and Pablo Báez

Library of Congress Control Number: 2025940180

For other books by Hoyt Rogers, please visit his website, hoytrogers.com

HEARD
IN
TITIAN

Nephews

By one of those eerie,
historic short-circuits,
my nephew's likeness recalls
Titian's daunting portrait of
Ranuccio Farnese, a
"cardinal-nephew"
who wasn't a nephew at all, but the grandson of a pope;
at twelve, not elevated yet, he wears the Malta insignia
as foreplay: just a boy, an ersatz knight, bewildered
by the silver cross, the oversize black coat, the gold
hilt of the hidden sword, the crimson brocade
with its white ruff and codpiece, as useless as
the crumpled glove he dangles from his hand,
obedient to his fate; though the snapshot here
depicts that mystery in a different mode:
centered on a massive overdose of cloth,
a child's expectant face, swaddled not
in consciousness like a new-born god
in a Virgin's arms, but only waiting for what
must come, the future that enfolds the fuller
body, allowing only the glaucous eyes, the red lips,
the blue, mismatched wings of a fragile collar, and
a small hand, powerless as Ranuccio's,

to surface now, while the loving waves
of the coverlet engulf the time to come,
though can't prevent the snowy billows
from shedding grey overtones
even as they hasten to protect
the boy from what
all of us must live.

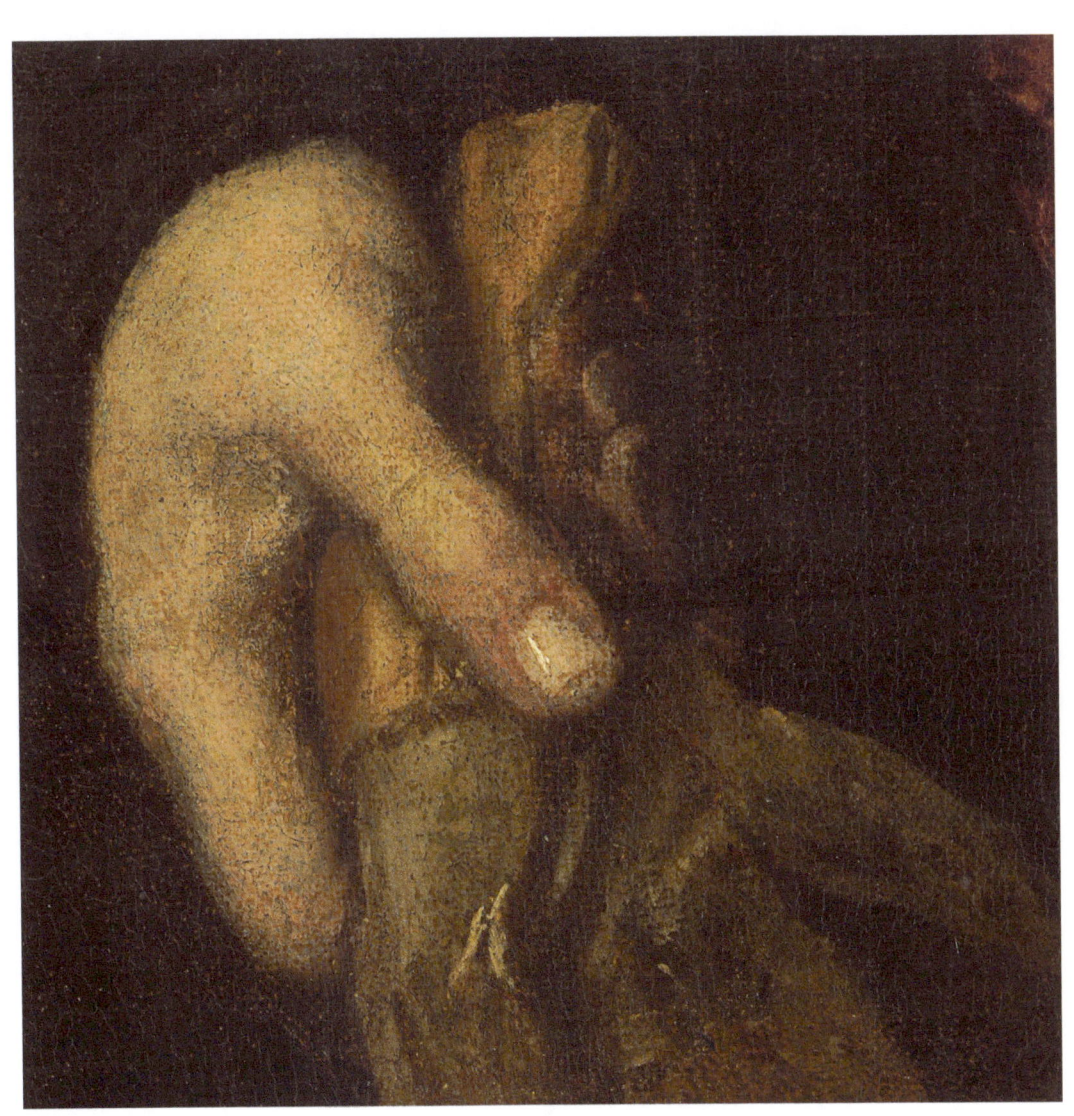

HEARD

IN
TINTORETTO

ICON

At San Marcuola
the table is static
as Leonardo's plank
on a fresco in Milan
its symmetry a throwback
with a cloth just unfolded
by Titian, flanked by caryatids
from Raphael, posed on a grey
shelf like Bellini's balustrades
to shield beholders from saints
though here a violation starts
with the naked foot wedging
discreetly into the bar to underline
that this is a Venetian church-floor
and not some whimsical Jerusalem,
a checkerboard of russet and cream
squared atop a stone schooner sunk
in the salt lagoon with only its deck
still visible above the lackadaisical waves
and here alone could Jesus and the twelve
dine in such alignment, not even St. John
breaking the profile with his head bowed
on the beloved's chest, since order reigns

around the central icon, encircled by rage
and fear in Sistine contortions, but himself
unfazed at the orbit's crux as dire shadows
fall in perfect rows and the children
silently point while the women bear
the bread and wine to their ordained
destination, and even the skeptic cat
is hieratic, as motionless and upright
as the ewer, yet these strewn benches
already betray you, dyer's boy, still
amassing robes of red ochre blue or
frosted brown in abstract whorls
for the euphoria of clotting light.

EARTHBOUND

Off to one side
at San Trovaso
not an icon any longer
but a narrative of floor
divided from floor, chapters
linked by windows or stairs
around the table's broken ellipse
tumbling to the left, apostles and
furniture askew with outrage and awe
as Van Gogh's plebeian chair topples
to the pavement of tiles stained by work
and dirt, since this is no palatial fantasy
by Veronese, some town of ideal forms
but an ordinary room, though faraway
a memory of divine anticipation
shimmers before the sky-stuffed
arch on a veranda where the ghosts
of Mary and Elizabeth unite forever
as the children kick in their wombs
and yet the foreground blocks their
joy, the surge of disciples with haloes
snuffed who beckon despair in floods
of muddied colors and threadbare clothes
around an earthbound Jesus, delivered up
by a Judas in red leggings, a malignant moon

that twists the tide to its climax, while above
on the highest steps who is she, servant
with a distaff or antique Fate scissoring
the thread, but who cares since the cat
keeps playing and a Renaissance page
stands in velvet of this year's crop,
a burgundy coat at center offers us
far into the future the salvific wine
and books strapped like a rucksack
in the corner brook no doubt
that the gospel of a homicide
will be proclaimed and a god
resurrected, verse after verse.

GAMEBOARD

At San Polo the marble tiles
are diagonal black and white
a gameboard rushing off the edge of
the room towards a landscape under
skies as vast as all creation, its temples
as fanciful as Veronese's—though here
they build not a setting but a beyond
where endless churches will transub-
stantiate the scene before our eyes, Christ
rising unexpectedly to hallow the cannibal
feast, dismembering his bones and flesh
into crumbs of bread, his blood recalled
only by the crimson that spills in a half-circle
to the right from sleeves to jackets to felt cap
to land on the sick man's trousers as he takes
the crust from an apostolic hand, his face like
the child's a bit swarthy, stagecraft "Moorish,"
as if they flowed from a Venetian's pipedream
of conquest by conversion, and there he looms
above them also marked by red, a lordly donor
posing as the servant's counterpart
at the other end, both of them aloof
from the turmoils of betrayal and death,

both foreseeing what will come as time
ripens the ears of wheat, and flour snows
from the waiter's sash to the robe and on
across the table-cloth
and the helper's back
to settle on the infant's
dazzling, upraised arm.

AUREOLA

No porticoes here, only walls
except for a window we open
by peering into this giant space
at San Giorgio, a tavern doubly
internal, as inmost as the shift
from static icon to this slanted
crossing-over, this illumined
night askew but symmetrical
between the celestial left
and the oblivious, fruited
right, the buoyant communion table
and the earth, Jesus blazing forth as
a sunburst at the crux, his aureola now
triumphant as the bread supplants wine
among the blank decanters, its crumbs
transmuted into bluish light that slicks
the cloth to metal, rising to Christ's cloak
and ricocheting from sleeve to robe along
the room, tying the muted sky of Mary
and Martha serving beneath the angels
to the sturdy calves and azure shoulders
of the worldly knave still denying a gift
of salvation, but there is where the future
unfolds, on a pavement no longer simply

Venetian, a pied design of faded red
yellow black and also blue, for faith
in the sublunar realm can only lose
its strength, even if seraphim wheel
equally around the sacramental lamp
and the inn's workaday rafters, watch
shady figures at the back no truth can touch
or Judas the blood-colored clown, but adore
the waiters who never presume
and the silent dog, not judging
the sly little tiger of a cat
just beneath the godhead
sniffing in the big basket
for a hidden mite of crust.

HEARD
IN
CARAVAGGIO

YOUTH WITH FRUIT

The real is offered, unashamed:
the flesh still callow, still naïve
despite the décolleté, the budding
mouth, the rosy skin entreating us
to love; a sturdy trunk, you brandish
glossy fruits, a grafted basket, spool
the light unraveled from a casement
improbably high, spin it back as figs
primly green or wantonly split, midget pears
on the branch, red-coquette or tawny-demure
and the big boys saffron too
twigged and bottoms-heavy
squatting low and fat, the ruby spill of pomegranate
seeds, medlars bletted for the spoon, apples splayed
brazen scarlet, sickly jonquil, or vermilion-striped
and sprawling grapes, deep magenta, bluish-black,
tarnished white, trumped by a lone two-tone
peach, flamboyant but like all these jailbirds
bound by plaited
wicker manacles
that grant only browning stems,
quizzical mint, vinous leaves to
overflow, and only one to say, blighted

and palm-down, what your listless eyes
and hair as somber as the wall, your marble
hand already meant: that brightness, strong
on your tough young fingers, moults to an ashen
sleeve, coils along your arm, back, shoulder, till
it winds you and all firm lushness
in a flaring, still unnoticed shroud.

YOUTH AS FRUIT

Deified, you preen as a cold defiler,
vaunt your wild corolla like a shout
to crown the end of innocence
with a backward mass, a table
set with wine and bread incarnate, flesh
as fruit, as flesh itself, the real presence
of seduction, your cere altar cloth
commingled with the pearly sheet
that writhes from your arm across your back,
tangles with the blue-striped pillow on a bed
and jumbles into your lap below the black
sash you open now, unloosening the silky
bow to elevate your sacrifices still unveiled,
the other shoulder, other bicep, other nipple
down to your navel and groin, as you recline;
though what your pink mask portends is not
desire but the solemn minuet of a pagan rite,
and like the leaves that frame your sightless
eyes, the jubilation swells from the molared
breakable dish, the deliquescent sigh of figs
and apples past their prime, an almost rotten quince,
a lusty verdant pear, a pomegranate stabbed to wolf
its peritoneal delights, and uninhibited the softening
grapes that plop onto the mensa linen, rise to mimic

your crimped hand, its dirty nails bunched to lift
a chalice of your aqueous blood, no mystery here
but evidence, exposited in the decanter's
shapely glass, its blowfish petaled mouth
as pursed as yours, your impassive face
only a bowl for the dark rapturous vines
that magnify the clusters
on the funeral slab below,
glowering with embers—crimson,
umber, garnet, jaundiced green—
the autumnal countersigns
to your bogus immortality.

FRUIT AS YOUTH

Your portrait needs no figure, only a warm
creamy space where someone's skin might
have bloomed for a moment, might have stirred
to the touch, since your textures, your perfumed
sweetness and sweat, your curving colors are all
here, and even your hidden succulence, your cry
of arousal, plenitude, satiated wilt: yes,
the sepia shelf where you now divulge
your inmost character has often held a glove,
a gold-ringed hand, a book, or pensive elbow
propping up a steadfast gaze; but your life is still
and visible in a sunny peach, faintly blushed atop
the isosceles mound, a crannied charcoal fig,
another rived and bister vying for center slot
with a pocked, xanthous pear, a nubile
brace to starboard, cozied stem to stern,
their frisky ridges counterbalanced by a plump,
stately quince, his physique outmatched in turn
by the ambrosial, bicolor apple your Eve
or Adam will bite, a bewitching carmine
cheek where a tiny, vanished snake has slyly bored
an orifice—suggestive of the rampant, juicy grapes
untrammeled by their woven pail,
spilling waywardly on every side

in dank profusion, golden, russet, indigo
and frosted white, virgin, ripe, climactic
or shriveling to decline, some but flaccid corpses
of what they were; and this the panoply of leaves
repeats like a spectral fanfare, haloing the fruit
despite disease and insect scars, raising a brief,
unvanquished anthem to an instant's fragility,
or descending into the skiff, already shades—
since you are honest, not symmetrical,
your shadows listing toward the night;
and yet you tell us more than a memento mori
as you cycle through the elements, earth-born
bodies aglow with the fiery orb, returning to air
in exhalations, starred with the dew of secretive
tears, because at every twist
we descry the bluish strokes
of skylights knowingly brushed
into your folds, the unseen you.

HEARD
IN
CLAESZ

WINDOW

Decanting like the lees
of embers, light ripples
inward, contracts and
swells till I transgress
a casement facing north
and purl along the cloth
on the table, even blacker
than the wall, to excavate
the frugal feast of olives
in a shallow bowl, bread
that flairs a white under-
side, contested to the left
by the foamy spiral
of the lemon's pith,
a ghost escaping
its rancid corpse
and the canary zest
brazenly twittering
an answer to the loaf's
fawn skull, its carcass
of extinguished wheat,
and in between I sparkle
from the mirrors I desire:
the embossed, golden handle

of the knife, its slender blade
a steely line to my reflections
in the silver platter's ellipses,
the florid rounds of the fallen
    pewter cup, until I ascend
    as a glorious body, gleam
    on the roemer's vitreous
    knurls, distorting myself
    in myriad refractions
    of fruit, metals, crust,
    wine, surging at last
    to the midmost brim
of the glass so I can vault
back through the window
    bright and small, an eye
beholding how my light
    and my shadow
    are always one.

TURKEY

All nature is dead
on this tablecloth,
white as a shroud
until the flesh dries out
and vestigial life is still,
the frame only a coffin
for abstractions, bone
or dust or circular pie
yet even here the feathers
spread in flightless wings
and I delineate their creamy,
dun, umber barbs and quills,
branching to the right
on grape-leaves, fruit
already bitten by decay
but spilling off a husky
Asia bowl, tilted to upstage
the humdrum pewter plates
of spices, lemons with comet-
tails carved by a showy knife
and humble oysters, mince
bursting from the pie-crust
and olives in a china saucer
meekly miming the brash

teal porcelain's brouhaha
but none of this will save
the breakfast's avalanche
into the chasm of grey walls
that know no procreant nuts
no bread no wine no opulent rug
and will admit only empty shells
exalted as the nautilus enshrined
in gold, the mollusc absent, void
like the turkey's sightless peepers
staring at a dog's inanimate snout
on the ewer where I limn a retreat,
warping forms on a bulbous belly
poised at the brink, vain
as the flower in the beak
of the gobbler,
so soon to wilt.

TIMEPIECE

I cannot hear, once I turn
into seeing, wed the light,
but I surmise the chimes
of a museum clock, just
as I alight on a pocket-watch
with its gold moon displayed
and blue ribbon dangling
a key-like fob at the edge
of the grey table
nicked, this time
as if mistreated by the years
but here a flower at the crux
though cut appears as frisky
as a lover's cheek, flapping
its leaves like both a nightingale
and lark to seesaw evening, day
and open with the walnut, crushed
to give birth, since you must know
a lone candle would not flood
such radiance on pewter discs
or underwrite with such deep lines
of shade the letter I address to you
my lost twin, Yoris or Yorick,
waxing red as a pilgrim's kiss

pressed to the page, my quill
sailing on the inkpot, briskly
glowing like my face
with its widened eyes
and aureate brow
as I invite you or
any soul to enter
my skull, to live.

HEARD
IN
VERMEER

PEARL

You turn to me
to ask who I am,
as if your candor
might be distrust,
though you confer
the turban's gloss
of yellows and blues,
the robe's ochre sky,
the white that sidles
into grey, the bogus
pearl where I mirror
myself, unperturbed
that you are an ideal,
a type, a cold cliché
with lips too scarlet
and lemur-like eyes,
an alabaster cameo
carved by my twin
the supple shadow
into cheeks, nose,
chin, brows, neck:
even so, I ask you
to question me

to let me touch
your skin, hear
me answer you
yes I am the seer
and you the seen
indivisible as we
quieten your fears
uncloud your gaze
brighten your face
into light
speaking
with light.

STREET

I trek from far-off
to tilt you slightly,
street of ruddy bricks
and weathered wood
on which I linger at noon
to watch my companions:
an aunt sewing at her door,
a neighbor pottering
in a sunny alleyway,
a young girl, yellow
on checkers of stone,
crouching to conspire
with a question-mark,
the blue clematis
daring to oppose
its bridal arabesque
to the prim shutters
of clotted oxblood, grey
or black-hinged celadon,
the smug walls and roofs
that invalidate the clouds,
stepping back in wedges
smudged with pale caulk

like water turning white
as I walk on each figure
and shingle, snoop
behind each crease
to see what secrets
you hide, but find
none at all, divine
no resistance here
to my patient,
forgiving eye.

MILK

We are alone in a room
where you serve no one
but yourself, and we crave
nothing more, nothing less
than a crust of time
and space, a crumb
of the bread-chunks
at rest on the table,
or the loaf lying plump
in its openwork basket,
round as yourself, your
arms and forehead and
waist, snug in the scullery
where I trickle like milk,
an officiant
who is light,
crowning your head
with a cap of white,
anointing your body
with royal blue, crimson,
yellow, and gilded green,
bidding the work-scarred
wall to swell with wicker
and brass, but granting

to you the deepest blue
that gleams from the other
jar, all over you and every
inch of cloth, that osmoses
into burnt umbers and reds,
tweaks Cupid and the fisher
on the cracked tiles
of a city we ignore,
happy to idolize
the foot-warmer
comforting you,
the earthen bowl
you carefully fill
as from the left
I rain my praise
since you alone
are the monarch
of this hour,
of this place.

VIEW

Cleared of rooms, of streets
we unleash the far-flung city
and the clouds, like clouds
ourselves above the shore
below us, drinking it till
we absorb its closeness,
the figures on mellow sand
not ladies or pensive maids
framed by plaster, jambs
but tiny, faceless ciphers,
and those along the quays
of the silent town no more
than specks hardly visible
across the reddish pewter
canal, its vague reflections
of steeples, turrets, or trees
softly blurred by a breath
of rippling air, even if all
the barges and stout ships
are motionless, their sails
furled, their black, curved
hulls sitting like old shoes
on a varnished, faded floor
we are painting once more,
reserving our prime and last
light for the sandbank below,
the farthest gables, stitching
blue, green, fawn, white, red

tiles and facades, to pinpoint
near as remote, there as here
even if
inching
to the center a bridge re-joins
what only seemed to lie apart,
and other arches mime
that mouth, aspiring us
like water under stone
so that we drift toward
the unseen, until a high
yellow wall updrafts us,
glimmers like a shard projected
from the beach, toppling ledges
of gold to the right that to the
left rise in a spire once again,
and we stare up at the clouds as
no one ever did along the lanes,
their woolly white suddenly graver
than the hard blue sky, their murky
prow surging forward like a word
we'd barely understood until now,
floating above what wilder sight
would dream, and we know this
same view unscrolls for us again
and again, exactly as it has, does,
and always will, stillness falling
slowly out of time until it settles
here into the grey water's sheen,
the never-changing page of glass.

LETTER

Every morning you stand
before this upper window
where I fall, if fall is not
for me too violent a verb
since I merely lean
over the sill to dew
your skin
with grey
and blue, to turn
this untidy table
the catty-cornered
chairs, naked wall
the picture-rod into
a placid azure lake,
and center you as sky
born anew from dead
mottled countries
on wrinkled maps
but then I seep
further inward
till I saturate
that shadow
you become

by rereading
the safe
ordinary
things I daily
write for you
in letters that blaze
from a nearby star
you see
as light.

FAREWELL TO DELFT

Above all, the sky. On the near shore, the light spills down, as golden as the sand. It rains on the horizon, too, but between near and far is a vast penumbra. The water can't mirror the sky's deepest blue, though a grey remembrance of it lingers there. The nascent waves glow opaquely, tinted russet by the roof-tiles, or charcoal by the city's facades. Radiance seeps from the clouds along roofs and walls—red, blue, yellow, green, beige, and brown. Only the farthest buildings shine. We're here on this shore and we're there, far off. To live our nearness is to live far-off, in equilibrium: this is the gift of perspective.

In the little street-scene you painted, where children play and women work, we easily ignore the clouds. But here we can't ignore them, since you've brought the sky up close: this interior is huge, and yet familiar as the furnished rooms you often depict. On the near shore, the figures stand out as individuals. Two women are chatting, and other people loiter nearby; but these aren't portraits. Their bodies are too small for that, though the space they occupy is infinite. Between the near shore and the far, we slowly lose our features, content to become like them. They are you and we are you, both near and far.

The black hulls lie at anchor, though their stillness moves. In a port, sails should be coming and going. Here, the ships resemble your clouds: suspended, they dilate, they grow. The faraway city surges forward, unchanged. The water ripples with the faintest of waves, arrested before they can form. The bridge that links the quays also holds them apart, just as the sun separates each brick within a single immobility. The people on the shore nearby us might be conversing. But how can we know? We can't hear them. Frozen, they stand in awe of the depth you let us see, with only that depth as your recompense.

The silence you've unveiled to us before, of women all alone in quiet rooms, is present in this endless view. You grant us a chosen instant, as vivid as the daily scenes we seldom register. Tiny citizens stroll on the distant walkways, unique but hard to decipher. We notice the town's arching gate; and under the bridge, an identical arch. Both bid us to enter, by foot or by boat. Lesser arches open, and windows dot the nubby facades like discreet invitations. Rooftops, steeples, masts, the crowns of trees—every surface glitters with specks of bluish white. Snowing, barely visible, they remind us to look at the sky.

NOTES

TITIAN

The poem compares a notable portrait by Titian with a casual snapshot of my great-nephew and namesake, so young he's still swaddled in a blanket. Ranuccio, a "Pope's nephew" (though actually the grandson of a Pope), was twelve years old when he posed in the oversized robes of a Knight of Malta. The commonality between the two images is the premise that our lives are "clothed" in their destiny from the outset.

The technique I've used for this and the following examples of ekphrastic verse relies on couplets and triplets of exactly equal length. The aim is to mimic how the eye takes in a canvas as a series of repetitions—similar themes, shapes, or tonalities—and yet all are delimited by an exigent frame. Commas, semicolons, colons, and dashes portray the pauses we make to absorb certain details, while still aware of the painting as a whole. The full stop comes only at the end, when we step away from the work.

Portrait of Ranuccio Farnese, c. 1542
National Gallery of Art, Washington

A celebrated dictum from the *Ars Poetica* of Horace, "ut pictura poesis" ("as is painting, so is poetry"), has guided writers for centuries. It has generally been interpreted to mean that they should offer the reader portrayals as detailed and lifelike as those of the visual arts. Long before the ancient Romans, Simonides of Ceos, the Greek lyric poet, had proposed a similar idea. "Painting is silent poetry," he declared, "and poetry is painting with the gift of speech."

Still, Horace's lapidary formula, so often cited, has proved more influential—especially in the Renaissance and Baroque—as part of a larger debate about mimesis, both in literature and in art. Yet it is not only nature or "reality" that they imitate, but each other as well: literature can engender art (usually, figurative art) and art can inspire literature. In a related device of rhetoric, ekphrasis, the author minutely describes an artwork, converting into words what the eye would normally see; the quintessential example is a passage from the *Iliad*, Book 18, where Homer "depicts" the ornate images on the shield of Achilles, fashioned by Hephaestus of bronze, tin, silver, and gold.

In our English-language tradition, several authors have dedicated magistral poems to individual artworks: Auden's "Musée des Beaux Arts" or Grace Schulman's sequence in *The Paintings of Our Lives* spring to mind. In my series of verses, inspired by four of Tintoretto's paintings, my purpose is somewhat different. Instead of shifting from the images to larger truths, I stay as close as possible to their surface details, while weaving in broader themes as I go. By doing so, I hope to help the reader bring these works into sharper focus, as variations on a theme: the Last Supper.

Successively, the versions at San Marcuola, San Trovaso, San Polo, and San Giorgio Maggiore portray the artist's quest to render the same scene in new terms. Looking at them intently, we can almost follow the movements of his mind, as though we were hearing him speak—while we remain the listening observers. At San Marcuola, the young painter seems to remember motifs from other masters: the grey parapet at the bottom of Bellini's works, the statuesque standing figures by Raphael, the symmetry of Leonardo's fresco in Milan, or the pleated white cloth of the suppers at Emmaus by Titian. In the ground-breaking image at San Trovaso, the earthiness of the sacred meal comes to the fore, in a setting that is almost plebeian. At San Polo, the upright donor and wide-open background imply the wealth and expansion of Venice's empire. In Tintoretto's final depiction of the Last Supper at San Giorgio Maggiore, the ghostly angels and the large-scale, slanted composition fuse the spiritual with the mundane.

The Last Supper, 1547
Church of San Marcuola, Venice

The Last Supper, 1566
Church of San Trovaso, Venice

The Last Supper, c. 1594
Basilica of San Giorgio Maggiore, Venice

CARAVAGGIO

When I take young people to art museums, especially those who've rarely been to one before, the painter they respond to immediately is Caravaggio. For example, Daniel, a twenty-something German-Italian-Latino friend, who was traveling to France for the very first time on a whirlwind tour, insisted on spending his one full day in Paris—not on a sight-seeing bus—but at the Jacquemart-André Museum. A favorite of Orhan Pamuk's (and mine), the collection focuses on Italian art: it boasts whole frescoes by Tiepolo, and other artists too numerous to name. In this instance, the curators had mounted the largest exhibition of Caravaggio canvases in history. After waiting in the frigid rain for two hours, we spent four hours before the paintings, and it was difficult for me to tear Daniel away. This tells me that Merisi embodies the spirit of our age better than any other master, old or new. His obsession with himself, reflected in countless self-portraits; his emphasis on violence and theatricality; his erotic ambiguity, which suffuses his art both sacred and profane—all these currents mirror the tendencies of our time, making him seem like an early twin of Francis Bacon.

At the center of *The Martyrdom of St. Matthew* in the Contarelli Chapel in Rome, a muscular executioner, almost unclad, dominates the scene, while a semblance of the painter observes from the left. I would hazard that the same semi-nude model poses for *The Flagellation of Christ* in Naples, this time with roles reversed; lost in a masochistic trance, he bears a subtle smile on his lips. Finally, I would suggest that he reappears in *The Deposition* at the Vatican; though dead, his body is corpulent and sinewy. Francis Bacon often created triptychs featuring the same model, especially

George Dyer. It's well-known that Caravaggio engaged in a similar practice, and not only in the case cited above; he regularly hired famous courtesans, such as Fillide Melandroni and Anna Bianchini, as well as certain rough characters from the street who recur in his works.

Another trio of paintings, from his early period, is the one I am presenting here. The subject is thought to be Mario Minniti, a sixteen-year-old, aspiring artist who apprenticed with Caravaggio in Rome, and later came to his aid in Sicily. I could have completed the triad with other canvases that feature him, such as the *Young Sick Bacchus* or the *Boy Bitten by a Lizard*; instead, I've chosen to underline the association of fruit with youth. In these ekphrastic poems, I highlight Merisi's willful subversions of iconography: his treatment of the still life as a sensual encounter, and of the Vanitas as an act of love.

Boy with a Basket of Fruit, c. 1593
Galleria Borghese, Rome

Bacchus, c. 1596
Uffizi, Florence

Basket of Fruit, c. 1596
Pinacoteca Ambrosiana, Milan

After eighty years of war with Spain, ending in 1648, the Dutch gratefully embraced their newfound prosperity. Wealth was conceived by many Protestant theologians as a sign of God's grace, as opposed to the benediction of poverty prized by Catholics. In part, this may account for the keen satisfaction with "the things of this world," the everyday life of the here and now, which characterizes art in the Netherlands during the Golden Age. As a very young man, Vermeer took up a mythological theme, striving to paint a "Diana at her bath," and yet the goddess and her attendants seem like sturdy peasants. Quickly enough, he found his stride, and painted the intimate domestic scenes for which we know him today.

All the same, generalizations like the above need a large dose of nuancing. Even in Italy, where lofty religious motifs (both Christian and pagan) had long predominated, an undercurrent of realism had come strongly to the fore in certain works by Annibale Carracci—and of course, in the entire oeuvre of Caravaggio, whether sacred or profane. Artists in Utrecht absorbed his influence so thoroughly that they could be said to form a "school," now known as the Utrecht Caravaggists. In Spain, the gods appeared among rough-hewn country folk, as in the Bacchic revel by Velásquez at the Prado. With the end of Spanish domination, hand in hand with the establishment of the Lutheran church, the lesser saints were gradually banned from Dutch painting, and yet purely Biblical themes remained in force. It would be wrong to assert that in the late seventeenth century, art in the Netherlands becomes wholly secular.

The Golden Age is still an era of profound belief. Even without explicitly religious motifs, the sense of the sacred is simply displaced into the "things of this world" themselves. At first glance, the still-life painting of the period may seem like the most down-to-earth of genres. But the more we contemplate it, the more we realize that spirituality imbues every canvas. This applies particularly to the Vanitas topos of which Pieter Claesz was a leading proponent. Its purpose is to remind us that human life is fleeting, and so we must turn our thoughts to God; if not, we will risk the loss of our salvation. While a skull is often present, as in the medieval theme of Memento Mori, Dutch painters multiply the evidence of ruin in other forms: sputtering candles, food decaying on a table, ancient books falling to pieces on a shelf, overturned glasses with their precious liquids spilled, watches that tick away until the hour of death.

In Romance languages, a still life is called a "dead nature": this is the essence of Pieter Claesz's art. Sometimes, as in the painting evoked in the first of my poems, his intent is understated in the extreme. Light turns into reflections, reveals itself as illusion, shades off into pitch-black darkness. In other cases, as in the second painting, a table full of dishes shows how excess leads to ultimate putrefaction. The warning inherent in the third painting is the most obvious and direct, with its timepiece, skull, and dying candle.

But when it comes to nature, we have to ask whether any vision we have of it may be called "alive" as opposed to "dead." Don't we automatically edit what we see, so that "nature" is always a series of pictures within our minds? If that is so, then ekphrasistic poems like these on Claesz take the phenomenon one step further, so that we witness existence from a third remove. The voices heard in his paintings become echoes within an echo. Yet they bundle together here in a single voice, that of the light itself, which moves through the paintings and singles out each detail. The lyric I becomes an eye.

Monochrome Still Life with Roemer, Tazza, and Lemon, 1638
Frans Hals Museum, Haarlem

Still Life with a Turkey Pie, 1627
Rijksmuseum, Amsterdam

Vanitas: Still Life, 1625
Frans Hals Museum, Haarlem

VERMEER

Though I had looked at Vermeer's paintings in art books from early childhood, at age seventeen I met them in person—the phrase seems appropriate, since they depict people at varying distances from the viewer, mostly close-up. First I encountered the pictures found today in Anglophone countries and France; later I got to know the ones I like best, all still conserved in the Netherlands. Five of the latter, two from the Mauritshuis and three from the Rijksmuseum, serve as the springboards for these five poems, *Heard in Vermeer*.

I use the term "springboard" because so much has been written about these canvases that there is little left to add beyond the reactions of each individual, by definition unique. In that sense, thousands of perspectives open up each day, as museum-goers examine the works; in addition, each renewed acquaintance with a Vermeer takes on another shading, according to the viewer's circumstances and moods. The lines here correspond to the words that took shape in my mind, sometimes quickly, sometimes slowly, as I contemplated the paintings for hours on end. As offshoots of visual art, they issue from the age-old tradition of ekphrastic poetry: the verbal imitation of artworks, as opposed to the natural world.

As I noted above in reference to Claesz, this begs several questions: Is any form of poetry based on "reality" as opposed to art? Don't we automatically edit what we discern? Isn't what we call "nature" merely a series of pictures within our brains from the outset? If that is so, then ekphrasis takes the phenomenon one step further, so we witness existence from a third remove. Of all artists, Vermeer provides the ideal portal for these successive stages of attachment and detachment. It has often been remarked that even his liveliest scenes appear arrested for all eternity. Despite the familiar objects and everyday occupations—pouring milk or reading a letter—they give the expression "still life" a whole new resonance. We enter this world in awe that it is so much like our own, yet subtly transfigured. The vanity of our ambitions falls away before the splendor of *being* itself, even if it is only an illusion. In Proust, the writer Bergotte feels overwhelmed by Vermeer's *View of Delft*; he focuses on a small yellow wall (or more likely, roof) at the moment of his death, convinced that it discredits his entire oeuvre. Less drastically, in the fourth poem of my sequence I evoke how that same sunlit patch "updrafts us," how it "glimmers like a shard projected/ from the beach." For me, it is quietly salvific, like everything painted by Vermeer.

Proust could aptly be called the poet of French prose, and his reverence for Vermeer is well-attested. As a rule, Francophone poets have devoted much more attention to the visual arts than their counterparts in our language. Baudelaire, often considered the father of modern art criticism, wrote extensively on Eugène Delacroix, the various salons, and humor in the arts. Mallarmé composed jewel-like "medallions" of Whistler, Manet, and Berthe Morisot; with Renoir, he was photographed by Degas. In our time, these poets' heirs (such as Yves Bonnefoy, André du Bouchet, and Jacques Dupin) have allied themselves with painters even more strongly—not only through essays on their works but also through hybrids of the graphic and the verbal, such as art-books or portfolios of engravings and texts.

Naturally, there are some important exceptions to what I just posited about English-speaking poets: Keats's "Ode on a Grecian Urn" would stand as the classic rebuttal to my assertion. In recent times, Frank O'Hara and John Ashbery authored many essays on art in catalogues and reviews. Like Keats, some of our contemporaries have devoted poems to individual works; Auden's "Musée des Beaux Arts" or Schulman's *The Paintings of Our Lives* (cited above in regard to Tintoretto) spring to mind. In Keats, Auden, and Schulman, images furnish a point of departure for broader verities, rather than the granular ekphrasis I have drawn from Vermeer (as well as from Titian, Tintoretto, Caravaggio, and Claesz).

Though I met Auden only once, I have known Grace Schulman for decades; without a doubt, her poetry ranks among the finest in our era. I sent her my Vermeer pieces as soon as I finished the first drafts; in our exchange of a dozen messages, she showed her usual generosity. She recalled that ekphrasis derives from the Greek verb "ekphrasein": to tell, to recount. "At times I feel the speaker is Vermeer," she noted; "at other times, the painting itself." In my reply, I explained the ambiguity as follows: "I suppose the original human viewer of the scene was the painter. But I wasn't concerned with the act of painting, more with what the light opens up to its own 'gaze'—and by extension, to ours."

After further discussion and several revisions, I sought to clarify that we who are looking at the work are the main protagonists. But because our engagement is so intense, we also identify with the painter, the subject, the shapes and colors, and even the light: strangely, our vision seems to suffuse the imaginary space like the light itself. As we concentrate on a painting, our awareness becomes enlarged and objectified. "While I don't want the reader to end up befuddled," I wrote to her, "I do want to retain that sense of a gradual widening from narrowness to infinity. If I can convey that to some degree, however modest, I will have reached my goal." In my own experience—often repeated—the viewer, the painter, the things depicted, and the luminosity of the picture merge into one.

Grace Schulman's words about my shifting lyric stance gave me pause. Unconsciously, by following the dictate of the paintings just as I saw them, I had stumbled upon their essence, as far as I was concerned: what I would call their visual polyphony. Each of them spoke to me in a multitude of voices that wove in and out of an overarching harmony—concomitant with the light, like colors refracted by a prism. The impression was enhanced by the fact that several times I visited the Dutch museums with fellow art-lovers, one from Venice and one from the Caribbean. An interlacing of comments—more like a passacaglia over a ground-bass of central themes—often unfolded as we stood before the artworks.

I remember Michele praising the extreme simplicity of Vermeer's technique in the *Girl with a Pearl Earring*, and how it relies on a limited palette an Italian might have spoiled, by saturating the tones with nuance. I remember him suggesting that because of its complex immobility, *View of Delft* offers us "a still life as vast as a landscape." I remember Pablo observing that the picture couples dark and light unevenly, in the radiance cast from above like a giant net. I remember him surprising me with the offhand statement that soon, the sky will tumble into the canal as drops of rain.

Of course, the voices I heard were all in my head, as soon as I pored over the canvases on my own. After I had written *Heard in Vermeer*, I returned to *View of Delft* only to discover that I still needed to explore it more thoroughly, like a country stretching off toward new horizons. Brick by brick, tile by tile, leaf by leaf, a glitter of pale blue seeps through the reds, yellows, and greens, as beaded as a wash of mercury. The city is dwarfed by the sky, which occupies well over half the picture-space: tilting upward, its blue gradations grow darker and darker, mimicking the white to cream to grey to black of the clouds. Paradoxically, the rain-clouds lean toward us as they surge above the cityscape, drawing us down into its hidden pools of light.

Delft floats between water and sky, both a workaday world and a celestial Jerusalem, much as it must have seemed to Vermeer. Ships unload their wares in the harbor, purveying the goods for merchants to buy and sell; citizens go about their business, pausing to chat on the quays. Even so, everything and everyone is only a reflection on the water; everything and everyone is just a spot or two of color, an apparition on the canvas. The painting is no more than some words heard in passing, suspended between then and now. Besides the fusion of earth and sky, light and dark, surface and depth, the fourth alloy Vermeer has forged is the most mysterious: the union of time with timelessness.

In retrospect, I felt moved to write a final ekphrastic poem—in prose rather than verse: "Farewell to Delft."

Girl with a Pearl Earring, c. 1665
Mauritshuis, The Hague

The Little Street, c. 1658
Rijksmuseum, Amsterdam

The Milkmaid, c. 1657
Rijksmuseum, Amsterdam

View of Delft, c. 1660
Mauritshuis, The Hague

Woman Reading a Letter, c. 1663
Rijksmuseum, Amsterdam

COLOPHON

This detail from *View of Delft* pinpoints the most likely candidate for the "patch of yellow wall" which overwhelms the writer Bergotte, precipitating his demise. Proust's description of the incident, in *La Prisonnière*, is thought to be the last passage he revised before his own death.

ACKNOWLEDGMENTS

Most of these poems were first published in literary reviews—
sometimes under different titles:

HEARD IN TITIAN ("Nephews") in *The Light Ekphrastic*
HEARD IN TINTORETTO, in *The Fortnightly Review*
HEARD IN CARAVAGGIO, in *Plume Poetry*
HEARD IN CLAESZ, in *Plume Poetry*
HEARD IN VERMEER, in *Mudlark*

I owe a sincere debt of thanks to the editors of all these journals for
their support and encouragement over the years.

"Farewell to Delft" appears for the first time in this volume.

Heard in Art is dedicated to my viewing companions: Pablo Báez,
Michele Casagrande, and Daniel Della Sala.